core belief ™

Bible Study Series
for junior high/middle school

THE TRUTH ABOUT

God's Justice

Group
Loveland, Colorado

The Truth About God's Justice

Core Belief Bible Study Series

Copyright © 1997 Group Publishing, Inc.

Credits

Editors: Amy Simpson and Lisa Baba Lauffer
Creative Development Editor: Paul Woods
Chief Creative Officer: Joani Schultz
Copy Editor: Debbie Gowensmith
Art Directors: Bill Fisher and Ray Tollison
Cover Art Director: Jeff Storm
Computer Graphic Artist: Ray Tollison
Photographer: Craig DeMartino
Production Manager: Gingar Kunkel

ISBN 0-7644-0862-3

10 9 8 7 6 5 4 3 2 1   06 05 04 03 02 01 00 99 98 97

Printed in the United States of America.

core belief

Bible Study Series
for junior high/middle school

contents:

the Core Belief: ▼God's Justice

Young people of every generation have at some time exclaimed, "Life's not fair!" But with just a *human* understanding of justice, those young people—and all of us—improperly perceive justice and injustice in the world.

Justice is the right and impartial treatment of others, and God is unique in his ability to determine justice—he set the standard and sees all things. He governs the world with justice. Because humans are sinful, our injustice separates us from God. But since God is merciful in addition to being just, he provides a way for us to have a relationship with him. Yet someone had to pay the price for our injustice: God punished Jesus Christ, the only sinless human ever to live, for our sins.

Yes, life's not fair. And aren't we lucky!

the ▼Helpful Stuff

the ▼Studies

▼God's Justice as a Core Christian Belief

When it comes to understanding God's justice, your young people face two dangers. They may fall into the belief that justice is simply a matter of opinion and that objective standards of right and wrong don't exist. Or they may look at the world's injustice and fall into despair because they see no way to overcome it. Fortunately, teenagers can avoid both pitfalls by learning what the Bible teaches about God's justice.

The more your young people learn about God, the more they'll see matters of justice from God's perspective. They'll understand that God loves justice and is committed to making the world a just place. With that understanding, your kids can go into the world as agents of God's justice, certain they're on the winning side.

This study course will help your kids develop a clear image of God's justice. First they'll look at the consistency of God's justice. As they come to understand that God's justice never fails, they'll gain a sense of God's desire that they overcome personal **racism.**

In the second study, kids will examine how God holds people responsible for the choices they make. As kids look at this aspect of God's justice, they'll learn to evaluate the consequences of **violence.**

Kids will then turn their attention inward to examine the tendency for **blaming others.** Through this study, kids will discover that life isn't always fair but that they can respond to God's justice by taking responsibility for their actions.

The final study of this course directs kids to examine the meaning and price of **compassion** and to test themselves to see whether they're willing to love their enemies. By delving into Jesus' teachings on responding to those who treat us poorly, kids can discover that although it may be difficult to display compassion, Jesus' example provides the clear standard.

God continues to establish justice in spite of our sin. He restrains the forces of injustice today and promises to institute perfect justice in the future. In spite of what we sometimes feel, God always has been and always will be just. And because God is just and loves justice, we should commit ourselves to being agents of God's justice in the world.

For a more comprehensive look at this Core Christian Belief, read Group's ***Get Real: Making Core Christian Beliefs Relevant to Teenagers.***

DEPTH FINDER

HOW THE BIBLE DESCRIBES GOD'S JUSTICE

To help you guide your kids effectively toward this Core Christian Belief, use these overviews as a launching point for a more in-depth study of God's justice.

- **Justice is the right and impartial treatment of others.** An action is right when it follows God's moral standard. That means we must treat one another the way God wants us to—without favoritism or prejudice (Deuteronomy 16:18-20; Psalm 82:3-4; and James 2:1-4).

- **God's character sets the standard of justice.** We don't have the authority to decide what's right and what's wrong. Instead, God's nature determines how we should act toward one another (Deuteronomy 1:16-17; 10:17-18; Matthew 5:48; and Revelation 15:3-4).

- **God governs the world with justice.** Even though we may feel that God has treated us unfairly, God always acts justly. However, God's justice may, on occasion, be delayed or hidden. And sometimes bad things happen—infants die, good people suffer—not because God is unjust, but because we live in a sin-cursed world (Deuteronomy 32:4; Nehemiah 9:33; Zephaniah 3:5; and Romans 3:25b-26).

- **God's justice takes several forms.** God promotes justice by giving equitable laws and ethical guidelines. God also provides various leaders whose responsibility it is to uphold the standards he provides. God also motivates individuals to act justly by rewarding righteousness and punishing sin (Leviticus 19:35-37; Job 38:12-15; Matthew 13:49-50; and Romans 1:18-19; 7:12; 13:1).

- **God balances justice with mercy to forgive human sin.** If God were only just, he would have to condemn us all for our sin. However, God chose to punish his own Son, Jesus, for our sin. As a result, God was able to extend mercy to us without compromising the demands of justice (Isaiah 46:12-13; 51:5; Romans 3:21-26; and 1 John 1:9).

- **Our injustice separates us from God.** Since God is just, he demands the same from us. When we cheat, lie, or take advantage of others, we sin and break our fellowship with God (Isaiah 1:16-20; 59:2-8; Jeremiah 22:15-16; Amos 5:14-15; and James 2:8-9).

- **God values justice more than acts of piety or worship.** God prizes truth, honesty, and impartiality so much that he refuses our "religious" deeds when we treat each other unjustly (Proverbs 21:2-3; Isaiah 1:11-17; Amos 5:21-24; Micah 6:6-8; and Matthew 23:23-24).

- **God wants justice to characterize individuals, groups, and social institutions.** Although we should treat each other fairly on a personal level, that isn't enough. We should also work for just laws and oppose unjust practices such as discrimination, oppression, and exploitation (Amos 2:6-7a; Micah 2:1-3; 3:1-3; Ephesians 6:9; and James 2:1-4).
- **Legal justice demands that everyone follow the law.** Leaders may not disregard the law to favor themselves or others. No one should try to subvert the law through lies or bribes; instead, everyone should seek to create a legal system that reflects God's standard of justice (2 Samuel 23:2-4; Psalm 72:1-4, 12-14; and Amos 5:12-15).
- **Social justice is more important than legal justice.** Even a "legal" act is unjust when it denies someone fair treatment. For example, it's unjust to take advantage of the poor or to show favoritism to the rich even if the law allows us to do so (Deuteronomy 24:17; Amos 5:11-12; 8:4-7; Luke 11:42; Colossians 4:1; and James 1:27).
- **Victims of injustice can cry out to God for help.** God is ultimately responsible for maintaining justice, so anyone being treated unjustly can ask him to intervene (Psalms 7:6-11; 26:1-3; 119:153-159; Hebrews 5:7; and 1 Peter 4:19).

CORE CHRISTIAN BELIEF OVERVIEW

Here are the twenty-four Core Christian Belief categories that form the backbone of Core Belief Bible Study Series:

The Nature of God	Jesus Christ	The Holy Spirit
Humanity	Evil	Suffering
Creation	The Spiritual Realm	The Bible
Salvation	Spiritual Growth	Personal Character
God's Justice	Sin & Forgiveness	The Last Days
Love	The Church	Worship
Authority	Prayer	Family
Service	Relationships	Sharing Faith

Look for Group's Core Belief Bible Study Series books in these other Core Christian Beliefs!

about core belief

Bible Study Series
for junior high/middle school

Think for a moment about your young people. When your students walk out of your youth program after they graduate from junior high or high school, what do you want them to know? What foundation do you want them to have so they can make wise choices?

You probably want them to know the essentials of the Christian faith. You want them to base everything they do on the foundational truths of Christianity. Are you meeting this goal?

If you have any doubt that your kids will walk into adulthood knowing and living by the tenets of the Christian faith, then you've picked up the right book. All the books in Group's Core Belief Bible Study Series encourage young people to discover the essentials of Christianity and to put those essentials into practice. Let us explain...

What Is Group's Core Belief Bible Study Series?

Group's Core Belief Bible Study Series is a biblically in-depth study series for junior high and senior high teenagers. This Bible study series utilizes four defining commitments to create each study. These "plumb lines" provide structure and continuity for every activity, study, project, and discussion. They are:

● **A Commitment to Biblical Depth**—Core Belief Bible Study Series is founded on the belief that kids not only *can* understand the deeper truths of the Bible but also *want* to understand them. Therefore, the activities and studies in this series strive to explain the "why" behind every truth we explore. That way, kids learn principles, not just rules.

● **A Commitment to Relevance**—Most kids aren't interested in abstract theories or doctrines about the universe. They want to know how to live successfully right now, today, in the heat of problems they can't ignore. Because of this, each study connects a real-life need with biblical principles that speak directly to that need. This study series finally bridges the gap between Bible truths and the real-world issues kids face.

● **A Commitment to Variety**—Today's young people have been raised in a sound bite world. They demand variety. For that reason, no two meetings in this study series are shaped exactly the same.

● **A Commitment to Active and Interactive Learning**—Active learning is learning by doing. Interactive learning simply takes active learning a step further by having kids teach each other what they've learned. It's a process that helps kids internalize and remember their discoveries.

For a more detailed description of these concepts, see the section titled "Why Active and Interactive Learning Works With Teenagers" beginning on page 57.

So how can you accomplish all this in a set of four easy-to-lead Bible studies? By weaving together various "power" elements to produce a fun experience that leaves kids challenged and encouraged.

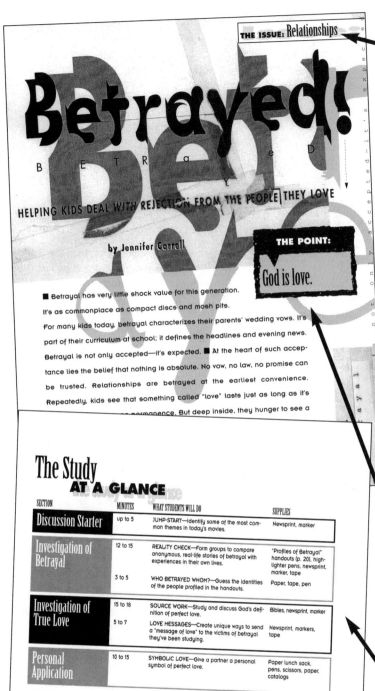

THE ISSUE: Relationships

Betrayed!

HELPING KIDS DEAL WITH REJECTION FROM THE PEOPLE THEY LOVE

by Jennifer Carrell

THE POINT:

God is love.

■ Betrayal has very little shock value for this generation. It's as commonplace as compact discs and mosh pits. For many kids today, betrayal characterizes their parents' wedding vows. It's part of their curriculum at school; it defines the headlines and evening news. Betrayal is not only accepted—it's expected. ■ At the heart of such acceptance lies the belief that nothing is absolute. No vow, no law, no promise can be trusted. Relationships are betrayed at the earliest convenience. Repeatedly, kids see that something called "love" lasts just as long as it's _____ permanence. But deep inside, they hunger to see a

The Study
AT A GLANCE

SECTION	MINUTES	WHAT STUDENTS WILL DO	SUPPLIES
Discussion Starter	up to 5	JUMP-START—Identify some of the most common themes in today's movies.	Newsprint, marker
Investigation of Betrayal	12 to 15	REALITY CHECK—Form groups to compare anonymous, real-life stories of betrayal with experiences in their own lives.	"Profiles of Betrayal" handouts (p. 20), highlighter pens, newsprint, marker, tape
	3 to 5	WHO BETRAYED WHOM?—Guess the identities of the people profiled in the handouts.	Paper, tape, pen
Investigation of True Love	15 to 18	SOURCE WORK—Study and discuss God's definition of perfect love.	Bibles, newsprint, marker
	5 to 7	LOVE MESSAGES—Create unique ways to send a "message of love" to the victims of betrayal they've been studying.	Newsprint, markers, tape
Personal Application	10 to 15	SYMBOLIC LOVE—Give a partner a personal symbol of perfect love.	Paper lunch sack, pens, scissors, paper, catalogs

notes:

● **A Relevant Topic**—More than ever before, kids live in the now. What matters to them and what attracts their hearts is what's happening in their world at this moment. For this reason, every Core Belief Bible Study focuses on a particular hot topic that kids care about.

● **A Core Christian Belief**—Group's Core Belief Bible Study Series organizes the wealth of Christian truth and experience into twenty-four Core Christian Belief categories. These twenty-four headings act as umbrellas for a collection of detailed beliefs that define Christianity and set it apart from the world and every other religion. Each book in this series features one Core Christian Belief with lessons suited for junior high or senior high students.

"But," you ask, "won't my kids be bored talking about all these spiritual beliefs?" No way! As a youth leader, you know the value of using hot topics to connect with young people. Ultimately teenagers talk about issues because they're searching for meaning in their lives. They want to find the one equation that will make sense of all the confusing events happening around them. Each Core Belief Bible Study answers that need by connecting a hot topic with a powerful Christian principle. Kids walk away from the study with something more solid than just the shifting ebb and flow of their own opinions. They walk away with a deeper understanding of their Christian faith.

● **The Point**—This simple statement is designed to be the intersection between the Core Christian Belief and the hot topic. Everything in the study ultimately focuses on The Point so that kids study it and allow it time to sink into their hearts.

● **The Study at a Glance**—A quick look at this chart will tell you what kids will do, how long it will take them to do it, and what supplies you'll need to get it done.

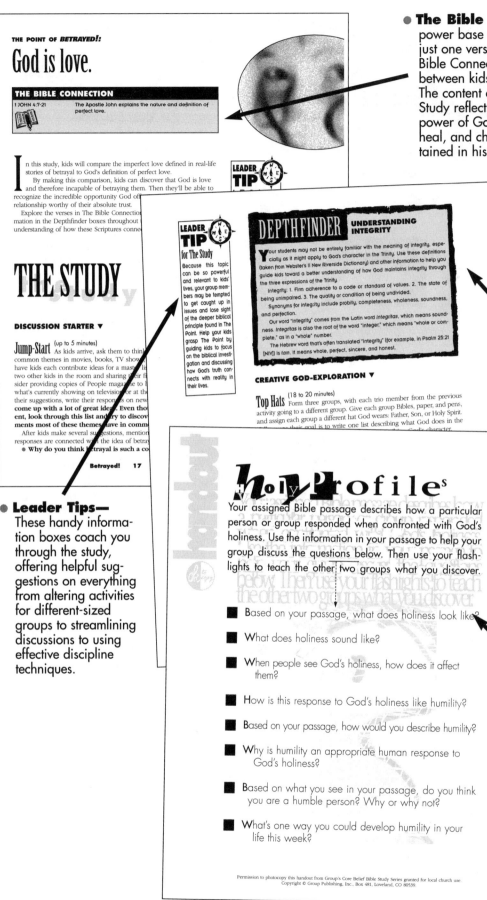

● The Bible Connection—This is the power base of each study. Whether it's just one verse or several chapters, The Bible Connection provides the vital link between kids' minds and their hearts. The content of each Core Belief Bible Study reflects the belief that the true power of God—the power to expose, heal, and change kids' lives—is contained in his Word.

THE POINT OF *BETRAYED!*:

God is love.

THE BIBLE CONNECTION

1 JOHN 4:7-21   The Apostle John explains the nature and definition of perfect love.

In this study, kids will compare the imperfect love defined in real-life stories of betrayal to God's definition of perfect love.

By making this comparison, kids can discover that God is love and therefore incapable of betraying them. Then they'll be able to recognize the incredible opportunity God of relationship worthy of their absolute trust.

Explore the verses in The Bible Connection mation in the Depthfinder boxes throughout understanding of how these Scriptures conne

THE STUDY

DISCUSSION STARTER ▼

Jump-Start (up to 5 minutes) As kids arrive, ask them to thin common themes in movies, books, TV show have kids each contribute ideas for a mast two other kids in the room and sharing sider providing copies of People maga what's currently showing on television or at the their suggestions, write their respon come up with a lot of great idea. Even the ent, look through this list and y to discov ments most of these themes have in comm

After kids make several su gestions, mention responses are connected with the idea of betray

● Why do you think etrayal is such a co

Betrayed! 17

● Leader Tips—These handy information boxes coach you through the study, offering helpful suggestions on everything from altering activities for different-sized groups to streamlining discussions to using effective discipline techniques.

LEADER
TIP
for The Study
Because this topic can be so powerful and relevant to kids' lives, your group members may be tempted to get caught up in issues and lose sight of the deeper biblical principle found in The Point. Help your kids grasp The Point by guiding kids to focus on the biblical investigation and discussing how God's truth connects with reality in their lives.

DEPTHFINDER   UNDERSTANDING INTEGRITY

Your students may not be entirely familiar with the meaning of integrity, especially as it might apply to God's character in the Trinity. Use these definitions (taken from Webster's II New Riverside Dictionary) and other information to help you guide kids toward a better understanding of how God maintains integrity through the three expressions of the Trinity.

Integrity: 1. Firm adherence to a code or standard of values. 2. The state of being unimpaired. 3. The quality or condition of being undivided.

Synonyms for integrity include probity, completeness, wholeness, soundness, and perfection.

Our word "integrity" comes from the Latin word *integritas*, which means soundness. *Integritas* is also the root of the word "integer," which means "whole or complete," as in a "whole" number.

The Hebrew word that's often translated "integrity" (for example, in Psalm 25:21 [NIV]) is *tam*. It means whole, perfect, sincere, and honest.

CREATIVE GOD-EXPLORATION ▼

Top Hats (18 to 20 minutes) Form three groups, with each trio member from the previous activity going to a different group. Give each group Bibles, paper, and pens, and assign each group a different hat that God wears: Father, Son, or Holy Spirit.

● Depthfinder Boxes—These informative sidelights located throughout each study add insight into a particular passage, word, historical fact, or Christian doctrine. Depthfinder boxes also provide insight into teen culture, adolescent development, current events, and philosophy.

Holy Profiles

Your assigned Bible passage describes how a particular person or group responded when confronted with God's holiness. Use the information in your passage to help your group discuss the questions below. Then use your flashlights to teach the other two groups what you discover.

■ Based on your passage, what does holiness look like?

■ What does holiness sound like?

■ When people see God's holiness, how does it affect them?

■ How is this response to God's holiness like humility?

■ Based on your passage, how would you describe humility?

■ Why is humility an appropriate human response to God's holiness?

■ Based on what you see in your passage, do you think you are a humble person? Why or why not?

■ What's one way you could develop humility in your life this week?

● Handouts—Most Core Belief Bible Studies include photocopiable handouts to use with your group. Handouts might take the form of a fun game, a lively discussion starter, or a challenging study page for kids to take home—anything to make your study more meaningful and effective.

The Last Word on Core Belief Bible Studies

Soon after you begin to use Group's Core Belief Bible Study Series, you'll see signs of real growth in your group members. Your kids will gain a deeper understanding of the Bible and of their own Christian faith. They'll see more clearly how a relationship with Jesus affects their daily lives. And they'll grow closer to God.

But that's not all. You'll also see kids grow closer to one another.

That's because this series is founded on the principle that Christian faith grows best in the context of relationship. Each study uses a variety of interactive pairs and small groups and always includes discussion questions that promote deeper relationships. The friendships kids will build through this study series will enable them to grow *together* toward a deeper relationship with God.

THE COLOR OF hate

COUNTERING TEENAGE PREJUDICE

by Pamela J. Shoup

■ For about a week, the United States was consumed with a six-letter word allegedly spoken by a police officer. ■ The word? ■ The "n" word. ■ When witnesses testified that Mark Fuhrman (a white detective who investigated O.J. Simpson's potential involvement in two murders) had used this word, the nation was shocked that such racist attitudes still existed in the land of the free. ■ Chances are, your teenagers weren't surprised. ■ They have to negotiate the maze of political correctness that often does more to reveal underlying racial tensions than to resolve them. Members of this nation's most ethnically diverse generation, today's young people daily experience the cultural and racial differences they can respond to with acceptance, unity, and appreciation or misunderstanding, division, and hate. ■ Your students need to know that God judges those who judge others, including those who prejudge others based on the colors of their skin. This study will help kids realize that God is the ultimate judge of all of us and that when his verdict is in, it's always right. His justice never fails.

THE POINT:

God's justice never fails.

The Study
AT A GLANCE

SECTION	MINUTES	WHAT STUDENTS WILL DO	SUPPLIES
Reflective Opener	5 to 10	SPEAKING FROM EXPERIENCE—Share times they've felt prejudice aimed at themselves.	Bibles, newsprint, tape, marker, slips of paper, pencils
Prejudice Experience	25 to 30	DISPELLING MYTHS—Experience prejudice based on traits assigned to them.	Bibles; yellow, red, blue, and green construction paper; safety pins; "Racial Myths" handouts (p. 23)
Unity Experience	10 to 15	WALL OF UNITY—Explore racial stereotypes and create a wall to symbolize the unity of all races.	Bibles, construction paper, markers, tape
Closing	5 to 10	COLOR BLINDNESS—Make and wear multicolored pins to show support for racial harmony.	Bibles, multicolored ribbon, safety pins

notes:

God's justice never fails.

THE BIBLE CONNECTION

MATTHEW 7:1-5; ROMANS 14:10-12	These passages tell us not to judge others because God is the judge of all.
JOHN 4:1-42	Jesus defies Jewish custom by talking to a Samaritan woman.
GALATIANS 2:11-16	Paul tells a story of Peter's prejudice.
GALATIANS 3:26-29	Paul explains that all Christians are unified in Christ, no matter their ethnicity or social status.

I n this study, kids will form groups and interact with other groups based upon prepared stereotypes. Then they'll create a Wall of Unity, describing positive traits shared by people of all races and ethnic groups.

Through this experience, kids can discover that God judges us when we judge others, including when we base our perceptions of others on their skin color, accents, or customs.

Explore the verses in The Bible Connection; then study the information in the Depthfinder boxes throughout the study to gain a deeper understanding of how these Scriptures connect with your young people.

BEFORE THE STUDY

For the "Speaking From Experience" activity, tape a sheet of newsprint to a wall of your meeting room.

For the "Color Blindness" activity, cut ¼-inch- or ½-inch-wide multicolored ribbons into six-inch strips. Make sure you have one strip for each student in your class.

LEADER TIP for The Study

Whenever groups discuss a list of questions, write the list on newsprint and tape the newsprint to a wall so groups can discuss the questions at their own pace.

THE STUDY

REFLECTIVE OPENER ▼

LEADER TIP

for Speaking From Experience

If your junior highers have trouble thinking of experiences when others held prejudices against them, have them think of incidents involving relatives or friends or something they remember from the news.

Speaking From Experience (5 to 10 minutes)

After everyone has arrived, say: **Today we're going to look at the issues of racism and prejudice. First let's define prejudice. What do you think it means?** Write kids' responses with a marker on the newsprint. If kids struggle with a definition, suggest a few dictionary-based ideas such as "judgment or opinion not based on fact" or "attitude of hostility directed toward a group or race."

Have students form trios, and then say: **In your groups, discuss a time you've felt prejudice against you—perhaps because of your race, your intelligence, your religion, your gender, or your family.**

After a minute of discussion, have each person write on a slip of paper the situation he or she shared with the trio, such as "I was called a name because of my race" or "Kids at school make fun of me because I make good grades."

Then have each trio read Romans 14:10-12 and discuss these questions:

● **Why did you think you were judged unfairly?**

● **According to this Bible passage, why will God judge us?**

● **How does this passage affect how you feel about the prejudice you experienced?**

After a few minutes, say: **People often treat one another in ways that hurt deeply. In Romans 14:10, Paul asks us why we judge and think we are better than others. He teaches us that only God can judge people and that <u>God's justice never fails.</u>**

Have kids tear their slips of paper into tiny pieces and throw them into the trash. Then ask:

● **How did it feel to tear up that prejudice?**

After students respond, say: **Let's explore tearing up prejudice in real life.**

LEADER TIP

for Dispelling Myths

If you have a group of seven or fewer students, do this activity with two or three color groups instead of all four.

PREJUDICE EXPERIENCE ▼

Dispelling Myths (25 to 30 minutes)

Say: **Most of us have felt some sort of prejudice, but how often have we shown prejudice to other people based on their looks or stereotypes we have about their race or ethnic group? Let's explore this by forming our own made-up ethnic groups.**

Have kids form four groups. Distribute one of the following colors of construction paper to each group: yellow, red, green, or blue. Then have group members safety pin one piece of construction paper to each other's backs. Give each group a copy of the three sections from the "Racial Myths" handout (p. 23) that do not correspond to its group color. For example, give the Yellow Group the "Red Group," "Green Group," and "Blue Group" sections. In their groups, have students read the stereotypes about the other groups.

After a few minutes, say: **I'm going to call out some situations, and I want you to interact with each other as if you were really in those situations. As you react, keep in mind the stereotypes you've read about the other groups.** Then call out the following situations one at a time, allowing kids thirty seconds to act out their responses:

● **You're all on a bus together.**

● **You're at a school dance.**

● **You're choosing teams in P.E. for a game.** (Have kids form four teams with one person from each group leading the team selection.)

● **You're walking on a dark street at night, and you meet another group.**

● **You see someone from another group on your "turf."**

Once the role-playing is complete, gather everyone back together, and give each group the section of the handout that describes their own group. After groups read their own descriptions, have kids turn to a partner to discuss these questions:

● **How did it feel to be treated a certain way just because of the color on your back?**

● **Is there anything true about the traits assigned to your group? false? Explain.**

● **Have you believed stereotypes about other races or groups? Why or why not?**

● **How does the truth that God's justice never fails affect how you treat people of other ethnicities? how you respond when people act prejudiced against you or a friend from another ethnicity?**

After the discussion, have kids form foursomes that include one person from each color group. Have each foursome read John 4:1-42 and discuss these questions:

● **How did Jesus break traditional barriers by speaking to the woman at the well?**

● **How did the Samaritans respond to Jesus' interaction with them?**

● **How did the disciples respond when they saw Jesus with the Samaritan woman?**

● **How would Jesus respond to prejudice in your school and neighborhood?**

● **How does Jesus' example affect how you'll treat people from other races or ethnic groups?**

● **How might the way you treat people from other races or ethnicities be an example to others?**

Say: **Jesus taught us and showed us by his actions that prejudice and racism are wrong. You can make a difference in the world by treating all people equally and by modeling Christ's love for everyone. <u>God's justice never fails,</u> and in the end he will judge those who judge others.**

LEADER TIP
for Dispelling Myths

This activity works best if you have an open space in your room where kids can sit or stand together as needed. Create an open space in the middle of your room by moving chairs, tables, and other furniture against the walls.

LEADER TIP
for Dispelling Myths

If kids are slow getting into this activity verbally, help them out by mentioning some of the stereotypes on the various lists. Encourage them to interact in a fun, but not mean, way. If you hear an inappropriate comment, steer the role-playing in a positive direction by mentioning one of the positive or funny stereotypes on the list such as the Yellow Group being happy and fun-loving or the Green Group liking the TV show *Dr. Quinn, Medicine Woman.*

DEPTH FINDER — UNDERSTANDING THE BIBLE

Jesus broke traditional barriers by speaking to the Samaritan woman at the well (John 4:1-42). Most Jews of the day wouldn't even travel through Samaria. They considered any contact with the Samaritans as defiling. So when the Samaritan woman happened upon Jesus at the well, she was surprised that he spoke to her. A Jewish rabbi would not have spoken to any woman in public, and he certainly would not drink from a Samaritan woman's cup.

John 4:4 says Jesus "had to go through Samaria." Biblical scholars interpret the phrase to mean that Jesus, as the Savior of all men, felt he had to minister to his people's enemies and confront the hate between the Jews and the Samaritans.

(Source: Frank E. Gaebelein, *The Expositor's Bible Commentary*)

UNITY EXPERIENCE ▼

LEADER  TIP
for Wall of Unity

Add to the prayer time by having kids write on the Wall of Unity names of people who've dedicated their lives to fighting prejudice and racism, such as Martin Luther King Jr., Cesar Chavez, Tecumseh, Harriet Tubman, and Harriet Beecher Stowe. Then have kids pray for the living relatives of these people.

Wall of Unity (10 to 15 minutes)

Ask:

● **Why do people hate other people because of the color of their skin or their ethnic background?**

Allow kids to respond. Then say: **Let's explore the colors of hate and racism.**

Have kids remain in their foursomes from the previous activity. Give each group markers and extra construction paper if needed. If you have seven or fewer students, give each person several sheets of different-colored paper.

Say: **On each sheet of paper, write some of the stereotypes you have about different kinds of people. Don't mention race, just traits. For example, on each sheet of paper write a word or phrase such as "lazy," "violent," "bigoted," "runs in gangs," or "dirty."**

After three minutes, have all foursomes who have blue papers share with the class what they've written on them. When all groups have finished reading, ask:

● **Are all "blue" people like this? Why or why not?**

Then repeat the process for those with red, yellow, and green papers.

Say: **All races have these traits. You can't judge one group by its color alone. There are good people and bad people in every race, ethnic group, and religion.**

In their groups, have kids read Galatians 2:11-16. When groups have finished reading, say: **Even Peter, who lived with and learned directly from Jesus, showed prejudice against people who weren't Jews.**

Then have groups discuss these questions:

● **What kind of prejudice did Peter show?**

● **What did Paul say about prejudice through this passage?**

● **According to Paul's teaching, how does a person become right with God?**

Say: **Now turn your papers over and write good traits about**

DEPTHFINDER UNDERSTANDING THESE KIDS

Many of your teenagers' parents and grandparents will remember the segregation of blacks in America, the civil rights movement, freedom marches and demonstrations, and Martin Luther King Jr.'s "dream." Other kids in your group may have families who emigrated from Asia, Mexico, Europe, and other parts of the world and had their own struggles with discrimination. Or you may have Native Americans whose families were displaced from their lands by settlers.

But all this is just ancient history to most kids. Your students live in the here and now and are writing their own histories. What are their views about racial issues? A Gallup Youth Survey published in Youthviews newsletter (November 1994) answers this question.

According to this survey, 56 percent of today's young people believe they are less prejudiced than their parents. When asked if they worry that they are too prejudiced, only 4 percent of kids answered with a strong affirmative, while 22 percent agreed somewhat.

Young Americans seem to believe that some cultural and ethnic differences may forever keep the two populations from understanding one another and achieving true equality. In response to the statement that whites will never understand blacks, 32 percent agreed and 66 percent disagreed. Thirty-three percent believe that blacks will never be truly equal in the U.S., and almost half of all black teenagers (47 percent) feel this way.

LEADER TIP for The Study

Because this topic can be so powerful and relevant to kids' lives, your group members may be tempted to get caught up in issues and lose sight of the deeper biblical principles found in The Point. Help your kids grasp The Point by guiding them to focus on the biblical investigation and by discussing how God's truth connects with reality in their lives.

people of all races, such as "kind," "intelligent," "loves God," or "works hard."

After a few minutes, invite kids to choose a wall of your meeting room to tape up their papers with the good traits showing.

When kids have finished, say: **Let me tell you a story about prejudice. A woman was driving through a neighborhood in a part of town unfamiliar to her. All she saw were faces of a different color, and she was getting scared. The people were pointing at her and shouting something. She was sure they were after her. Pretty soon she saw a street sign and realized she was driving the wrong way on a one-way street—the people were merely trying to tell her she was in danger** (Studs Terkel, *Race: How Blacks & Whites Think & Feel About the American Obsession*).

Invite kids to share their experiences of having a prejudice proven wrong. Then say: **God created all men and women equal. Racial prejudices and stereotypes are man made, and God judges those who judge others. God's justice never fails.**

Everyone say a silent prayer asking God for forgiveness for your own prejudice. Ask for the strength and wisdom to overcome prejudice and racism.

Then have kids share with their foursomes the actions they'll do in the coming week to show kindness to a person of another ethnic group. Invite kids to express to the whole class what they intend to do to show kindness and respect to someone different from them.

LEADER TIP for Wall of Unity

In case your students can't come up with a time when they held a wrong prejudice about someone, be prepared to share an experience of your own or of someone you know well.

LEADER
TIP
for Color Blindness

Have kids further encourage each other by allowing them to write their partners' names and their encouragements on pieces of construction paper on the Wall of Unity.

CLOSING ▼

Color Blindness
(5 to 10 minutes)

Have kids close their eyes as you read Matthew 7:1-5 aloud to them. Ask:

● **What does this Scripture tell us about ourselves and about judging other people?**

● **How easy would it be to judge another person based on looks when you have your eyes closed?**

Have kids open their eyes. Ask:

● **According to this Bible passage, how can we overcome racism and prejudice?**

Say: **This Scripture tells us that God will judge us in the same way we judge other people and that <u>God's justice never fails.</u> Let's make ribbon pins to show our commitment to racial harmony.**

Distribute safety pins and the ribbon pieces you cut before the study. Have kids fold ribbons into loops and hold them together with pins. (To save time, loop and pin the ribbons before class.) Tell kids to find partners and pin each other's ribbons on, then tell their partners what they like or admire about them.

RACIAL MYTHS

Yellow Group

Your group is lazy. You work only when necessary and try to avoid doing any work at all. You love broccoli, which all the other groups hate. You like to wear cowboy hats. You are less intelligent than the other groups. You are a happy, fun-loving people who like to party. All the other groups hate you because you always wear yellow.

Red Group

Your group is sneaky and dishonest. You are intelligent and use your intelligence to plot against other groups. You eat lots of Brussels sprouts, which the other groups hate. You are good athletes, but your favorite sport is Ping-Pong. You often travel in gangs and cause trouble. You always wear red, which the other groups hate.

Green Group

People in your group are irresponsible. You have no desire to better yourselves and do not mind living in poverty and filth. Your people love to eat avocados, which the other groups hate. Your favorite TV show is *Dr. Quinn, Medicine Woman*. People in your group often speak their own language and keep to themselves, but your language is beautiful and musical. You are a musically talented people who sing and dance well. You always wear green, which the other groups hate.

Blue Group

People in your group are treacherous and can't be trusted. You're good liars and have been known to murder people. Blues love to eat onions, which the other groups hate. You all wear blue tennis shoes. Your people will do anything to get their hands on liquor and are notorious drunks. Your group makes its own beautiful clothing, mostly blue, which the other groups hate.

Someday You'll Pay

Helping Kids Escape the Trap of Violence

by Meredith TeGrotenhuis

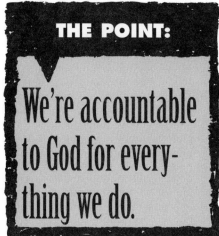

THE POINT:

We're accountable to God for everything we do.

■ What's happening in our society is frightening: Our streets aren't safe, homes have become places of fear, and schools are battlegrounds. For some, a jail sentence is a mark of achievement; a prison term, a medal of honor. Consequences are irrelevant and meaningless, justice is relative and temporal, and responsibility is a joke. Violence is a trend, and fear has become a way of life. ■ You and your students may face violence every day, or you may feel that its problems are thousands of miles away. But the spirit of violence is pervasive—no matter where you live. ■ This study focuses on the ramifications of violence in society and challenges students to contemplate the consequences of their own decisions and actions in light of God's ultimate judgment.

The Study
AT A GLANCE

SECTION	MINUTES	WHAT STUDENTS WILL DO	SUPPLIES
Simulation	30 to 40	THE YEAR 2027—"Transform" into a society plagued with gang violence and maneuver through a series of decisions that may save or destroy civilization.	Armbands as described in the "Before the Study" box (p. 27), flashlights, "Group Descriptions" handouts (pp. 35-36), scissors, slips of paper, paper, pencils or pens, bell or whistle
Reflection	5 to 10	BACK TO THE PRESENT—Discuss what happened during the simulation.	
Bible Discovery	5 to 10	REALITY CHECK—Explore Scriptures that illustrate justice and accountability and symbolically pay for their own actions.	Bibles, paper, pencils or pens, slips of paper, markers
Challenge	up to 5	THE REAL WORLD—Be challenged to acknowledge God's justice and accept God's grace.	Bible

notes:

We're accountable to God for everything we do.

THE BIBLE CONNECTION

PSALM 7:10-17   David comforts himself in knowing that because of God's justice, evil digs its own grave.

EZEKIEL 18:25-32   Ezekiel warns the Israelites that God will judge them according to what they do.

I n this study, kids will participate in a simulation that introduces the relationship between actions and consequences. Then kids will connect their own experience to what David and Ezekiel said about God's justice.

Through this experience, kids can discover that God holds them responsible for their actions and that violence has a price.

Explore the verses in The Bible Connection; then examine the information in the Depthfinder boxes throughout the study to gain a deeper understanding of how these Scriptures connect with your young people.

BEFORE THE STUDY

For the "Year 2027" activity, create armbands to designate five groups the kids will form. You can cut a sheet into strips and mark the strips with various colors, cut out various colors of construction paper or yarn, use adhesive name tags, or buy small sections of fabric from the bargain table at a fabric store and cut them into strips. You'll need one armband for each student. Also photocopy the "Group Descriptions" handout (pp. 35-36) and cut apart the descriptions. Make sure you have one description for each student.

LEADER TIP
for The Study

Because this topic can be so powerful and relevant to kids' lives, your group members may be tempted to get caught up in issues and lose sight of the deeper biblical principles found in The Point. Help your kids grasp The Point by guiding them to focus on the biblical investigation and by discussing how God's truth connects with reality in their lives.

THE STUDY

SIMULATION ▼

The Year 2027 (30 to 40 minutes)

As students arrive, give each a color-coded armband you created before the study. Each color or design designates one of the following groups for the simulation: Sovalos, Kyats, Government, School System, and the Public. Try to assign at least one adult leader to each group. So groups don't begin acting out their parts too soon, don't tell kids their group designations until you've separated them into groups and introduced the simulation activity.

After everyone has put on an armband, turn out all the lights except for a flashlight. Put the flashlight on the floor in the front of the room with the beam of light pointing up. Stand above the beam of light so it lights up your face and allows you to read. When everyone is quiet, say: **The year is 2027. Gang warfare has exploded in the last twenty-five years. Ninety-five percent of people between the ages of fifteen and fifty carry weapons; 25 percent of those people carry automatic machine guns.**

There are five main groups of people in society: the Sovalos, the Kyats, the Government, the School System, and the Public. The Sovalos and the Kyats are gangs. They're sworn enemies who have terrorized the Public with endless acts of random violence and revenge killings. The School System is on the verge of collapse. The teachers keep quitting because of the violence in their classrooms, and the administration is running out of money. The Public is frustrated with the School System for messing up their kids and with the Government for not stopping the violence. The Government has less control every day.

All urban and suburban areas have been claimed by one gang or the other. In the inner cities of the United States, it is no longer safe for anyone to walk the streets. Most of the buildings have been claimed by the gangs, and they shoot anyone walking on the streets below. It is literally a war zone. Street battles are a weekly ritual. Gangs converge on the inner city every Monday night. The gunfire begins about midnight and continues until dawn on Tuesday. Each week's death toll is higher than the week before. Seventy-five percent of Americans under the age of twenty-five belong to either the Sovalos or the Kyats. If you don't belong to a gang, you're attacked for being a "resister." Statistically, your chances of survival are better if you belong to a gang. In the schools, the dropout rate is 43 percent. Most of the remaining students carry guns to school every day, even though the administration doesn't allow it. The playgrounds and campuses are marketplaces for hard-core drugs and are centers for gang

DEPTH FINDER — VIOLENCE IN THE BIBLE

Violence gets mixed reviews in the Bible. In some places, it is categorically condemned and punished, but in other places it's ordained by God. How do we know whether violence is right or wrong? The church has been debating this point for hundreds of years. If you want to join in the debate, here are some key Scripture passages:

Genesis 6:11-13	God told Noah that God would destroy the earth and all people because of their violence.
Exodus 13:15	In response to Pharaoh's refusal to release the Israelites from Egypt, God put to death every firstborn male in Egypt.
Joshua 8	God instructed Joshua and the Israelites to ambush the army of Ai and kill everyone who lived in the city—men and women.
Judges 4	God ordained Deborah to lead the Israelites in destroying the Canaanite army.
Ezekiel 7:23-27	God warned the people of Israel that disaster and suffering would come because they had behaved violently.
Zephaniah 1:14-18	God described a day when his judgment would be violently carried out against people.
Romans 12:17-21	Paul admonished Christians to live lives of peace, trusting God to punish those who do wrong.
1 Timothy 1:12-14	Paul confessed his history of being a violent man and thanked Christ for his grace and mercy.

LEADER TIP for The Year 2027

OK. So you've started the simulation, everything is rolling along, and then your students start making decisions that force you to take action. What do you do? Here are some possible scenarios and some questions you should think through:

If the Sovalos decide to fight but the Kyats don't, how much territory do the Sovalos gain? five blocks? ten blocks? What if the Kyats decide to fight too? Which gang wins territory—and how much?

What if the Government decides to sacrificially cut its own paychecks? How soon do families run out of money? in one day? two?

What if the Government decides to cut school funds? When does the electricity get turned off in the schools? If the Government decides to cut the military, does another country take advantage and invade?

What if the School System chooses to strike? How soon do teachers' families run out of money? What if teachers decide to start screening every student entering schools? Does it work? Is there a student riot?

What if a group decides to dissolve and leave the country for greener pastures? What happens to them? Are they able to leave the country when everything is in chaos? Are there flights out of the country?

What if the gangs decide to unite against the Government? Do they succeed in their takeover attempt? Does another country invade?

---

recruitment. The only teachers left either are too stubborn to give up or are controlled by the gangs.

It is Monday night. The weekly battle will begin in two hours, the Government has no money and may have to cut funding for schools, the teachers have threatened to strike, and the Public is outraged.

Your decisions will determine what happens. Will another fight take the lives of more young people? Will the School

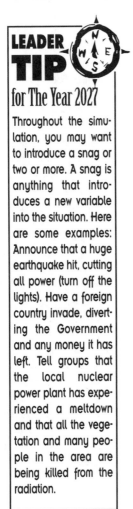

LEADER TIP for The Year 2027

Here are some sure signs that you should end the simulation:

● Only two groups are left intact, and they contain less than 60 percent of your students.

● It's too chaotic to continue.

● The groups are making random, silly decisions—for example, the teachers decide to commit mass murder in the classrooms.

LEADER TIP for The Year 2027

Throughout the simulation, you may want to introduce a snag or two or more. A snag is anything that introduces a new variable into the situation. Here are some examples: Announce that a huge earthquake hit, cutting all power (turn off the lights). Have a foreign country invade, diverting the Government and any money it has left. Tell groups that the local nuclear power plant has experienced a meltdown and that all the vegetation and many people in the area are being killed from the radiation.

System shut down, forcing kids out into the street? Will the Government dissolve into chaos, or will it survive on a thread? Will the violence ever stop?

In your groups, you'll decide on the next action you'll take. Each group will get a group description to help it decide what to do—but the choice is up to you. Remember: <u>We're accountable to God for everything we do.</u>

You need to do three things in your group: Read your group description, make a decision about how your group is going to respond to the situation you face, and appoint a reporter who will bring your decisions to me. As soon as you've made your first decision concerning what to do, the reporter for your group will write the decision on a slip of paper and bring it to me, the editor of the newspaper. I will announce the decision and its consequences to all the groups. You can respond to each other's decisions as they're announced.

Turn on the lights (if possible, turn on only a few), and instruct the students to congregate in their separate groups along the walls of the room. Give each person his or her group's description from the "Group Descriptions" handout (pp. 35-36). Give each group a flashlight, several slips of paper, and a pencil or pen.

While students are reading their descriptions and discussing their roles, walk around to each of the groups, answering any questions. Be careful not to say too much—let groups struggle and ponder their options for a while. You may suggest that groups examine their goals.

As groups begin to make decisions, it's vital to let the consequences of their decisions play out. Let kids respond naturally to each other and to decisions.

When each group has had several minutes to read its description and discuss its role, begin the simulation. Instruct groups to decide on their next course of action. As you lead the simulation, be aware that as the leader, you have these four jobs:

● As editor of the newspaper, you are the hub of communication between groups. Each group will decide on an action, and the group reporter will write it down and bring it to you. You will then decide when to tell the other groups what action a group has decided to take. For example, the Sovalos may decide to fight, but it would not be appropriate for the Kyats to know that information until "midnight." In that case, you would need to withhold that information until you announce "midnight." That's when your second job comes in.

● As time passes, you'll announce to everyone in the room what action is taking place (like a true newspaper editor), and then you will have to quickly determine the consequences of the decisions the groups make. For example, if both gangs decide to fight, you must decide how many are killed and who "wins" the battle; if the Government decides to bring in the military and the gangs decide to fight back, you must decide whether the military gains control or the gangs are successful; if the teachers go on strike, you must decide when families run out of money because mom or dad isn't bringing home a paycheck. When making your decisions, make them as true to life experience as possible, while not allowing groups to solve the problems easily. Remember: Life isn't fair, so your decisions don't have to be either. If you have an extra adult leader, you may want to employ him or her as your co-editor to help you make decisions.

● You will keep and announce "simulation time," letting time pass at even intervals so that one group isn't operating on Friday afternoon when another is still on Monday night. For example, after a period of time, announce, "It is now midnight." Then after another period of time, say, "It is now Tuesday morning." There may be a lag for some groups after they have made decisions and before the action takes place. During this time, they should talk about other options and anticipate their next move. Allow adequate time for groups to make decisions, but not too much time. Remember: Split-second decisions exist in real life; they should exist here, too. You may choose to add some tension by accelerating "simulation time" as the game progresses.

● You'll moderate any meetings between groups. If one of the groups wants to meet face-to-face with another group, bring both groups to the middle of the room and monitor their discussion. For example, if the Government wants to meet with the School System to work out a possible alliance, you must be present to make sure the discussion is realistic and stays under control. You might use a table to maintain physical distance between the groups.

When the simulation has reached an appropriate stopping place or when thirty minutes has passed (whichever comes first), get everyone's attention by ringing a bell or blowing a whistle. Say: **To conclude this simulation, gather in your original groups, and write a prayer to thank God for the other groups and what you learned from them. Write one sentence for each group in the simulation.** Give each group a piece of paper.

When groups have written their prayers, have kids form one circle; then have a spokesperson from each group read the prayer the group wrote.

REFLECTION ▼

Back to the Present
(5 to 10 minutes)
Have kids remain in a circle and sit down. Say: **Now it's time to move from the imaginary world to the real world. In that simulated world we created, our actions had simulated consequences; in the real world, we have real consequences. In fact, <u>we're accountable to God for everything we do.</u>**

Ask:

● **What was violent about the simulation?**

● **Did you like the violence in the simulation? Why or why not? Was it fun? Why or why not?**

● **How do you think other people felt about the violence in the simulation?**

● **Do you think the violence in this experience seemed to affect some people more than others? Why or why not?**

● **What do you think would have been the results of this simu-**

LEADER TIP
for The Year 2027

Groups may be tempted to write their own "press releases," including not only their decisions but the consequences as well. For example, the Kyats may send a report saying, "Kyats assassinate top government official." Actually, they only decided to *attempt* the assassination. You get to decide if they succeed. Don't let them get away with writing their own destinies!

Also be careful of making decisions for a group in your own announcements. For example, if the Government decides to send ambassadors to the gangs and you announce that the ambassadors were shot on sight, you made the decision for the gangs to shoot. It's their responsibility to react to other groups.

If a group is slow or stubborn, don't force it to make a decision. If a group doesn't make a decision, that *is* the decision, and the group will reap the consequences!

"Death" is tricky. If your students "die" and leave their groups, almost everyone may end up sitting in the "dead" group with nothing to do. You may want to institute "hypothetical death" so your students aren't the actual victims; instead, hypothetical people would "die" (imaginary gangsters, government officials, and teachers). In this case, your groups would remain relatively intact and students could stay involved.

LEADER TIP
for Back to the Present

Simulations are unpredictable. When it comes to discussing a simulation experience, it's important that you discuss specific experiences. The questions provided are generic and only cover the basics; use these as a springboard to talk about specifics. For example, if the Government decided to abandon ship and nuke the city, ask the following questions during the discussion time:

● Why do you suppose the Government chose to nuke the city?

● How did you react to that?

● What were the consequences of their actions?

lated violence in real life?

● **What decisions do you feel good about? Why?**

● **What decisions do you feel bad about? Why?**

● **How did your decisions affect what happened?**

● **What would you do differently if we could do the simulation again?**

● **What would God say about the decisions you made?**

Say: **All our actions and decisions have consequences. Sometimes we think we've gotten away with something, and sometimes we see clear consequences to our actions. Sometimes life is fair, and sometimes it isn't. But we're accountable to God for everything we do.** Ask:

● **What does it mean to be accountable?**

When students have had a chance to respond, say: **One dictionary defines "accountable" as "obliged to account for one's acts" or "responsible."** Ask:

● **What does it mean to be responsible?**

● **What did the actions and consequences in our simulation experience teach you about accountability?**

● **How realistic do you think this simulation was?**

● **How does this simulation experience relate to your everyday life?**

● **What does this experience show about the effects of violence?**

Say: **If you baby-sit, you are responsible for that child. If you hit your brother, you are responsible for any bruises. If you cheat on a test, you are accountable to the teacher for your actions. And we're accountable to God for everything we do. Even though violence may seem fun or harmless, it always has consequences. When we behave violently, our behavior affects other people, we suffer consequences, and God ultimately holds us accountable.**

"He who is pregnant with evil and conceives trouble gives birth to disillusionment. He who digs a hole and scoops it out falls into the pit he has made. The trouble he causes recoils on himself; his violence comes down on his own head."—Psalm 7:14–16

Ezekiel's ministry to the Israelites (592-570 B.C.) took place in the midst of chaos in the Middle East. The Assyrians conquered Israel (the Northern Kingdom) around 722 B.C., and Judah (the Southern Kingdom) had been under Egyptian rule since 609 B.C. Babylon conquered Egypt, and in 597 B.C. the king of Judah revolted against the Babylonians. Babylon squelched the rebellion and by 586 B.C. had carried the people of Judah off to captivity in Babylon.

Ezekiel's role as prophet and priest made him the bearer of bad news. He continually reminded the Israelites that the ruin of Jerusalem and the temple was a result of their own disobedience. God was holding them accountable for their actions!

Ezekiel 18:25-32 lies within a larger passage in the book that speaks to personal accountability. God told the people that he would judge them individually on the basis of their actions. In other words, they wouldn't be able to ride on the coattails of their righteous parents anymore. Ezekiel repeated, "The soul who sins is the one who will die" (verses 4 and 20). In God's eyes, this is justice: personal accountability for sin and disobedience.

BIBLE DISCOVERY ▼

Reality Check (5 to 10 minutes)

Say: **Let's look at what God says about our decisions and our actions. But first let's pray for our discussion.** Have a volunteer offer a one-sentence prayer, asking God to guide the discussion.

Have students form groups of five or six, with at least one member from each simulation group in each small group.

Give each group Bibles, paper, and a pencil or pen. Have groups read Psalm 7:10-17 and Ezekiel 18:25-32. Then have each group come up with a slogan or a cheer that sums up both passages. Then have groups discuss these questions and write down their answers:

● **According to these Scripture passages, how does God respond when people do wrong?**

● **What do these passages say about the choices we make?**

● **What are some biblical examples of God's judgment on the "wicked"?**

● **When in your life have you had to "pay" for your actions?**

● **Do you think the message of these passages applies to you and your actions? Explain.**

When groups have discussed the questions and written their answers, have each group tell the rest of the students its slogan or cheer and then its answers to the discussion questions.

Next give each person a blank slip of paper the size of a dollar bill. Make markers available, and instruct each student to design a "dollar bill" that illustrates one way he or she has had to "pay" for actions in the past. For example, if cheating on a test cost a student an A in a class, he or she could illustrate a report card with an A on it. Or if shoplifting cost a student peace of mind even though he or she was never caught, the student could illustrate a happy face.

When students have finished designing their dollar bills, have each person find a partner. Instruct partners to share their designs with each other, explain what their designs mean, and then hand over their dollar bills to each other, representing the "payment" they've made for their actions.

Ask:

● **How did this activity illustrate the fact that <u>we're accountable to God for everything we do?</u>**

● **What did accountability mean for you in the specific situation you described to your partner?**

CHALLENGE ▼

The Real World (up to 5 minutes)
Read Ezekiel 18:30-32 aloud, substituting your youth group's name in place of the references to Israel. Say: **God tells us that <u>we're accountable to him for everything we do.</u> God is just; he will give everyone what they deserve. But that's not the end of the story! Jesus died, so we aren't tied to our sin. We can repent and live!** Offer a short prayer asking God to guide each person in the group to make good decisions. You may want to make yourself available after the study to talk with students who have questions about what it means to repent and be forgiven.

Group descriptions

Photocopy this page, cut apart the descriptions, and give the appropriate description to the members of each group in the simulation experience.

Sovalos

You're a gang member, and you shoot anyone for almost any reason. Your goal is to get rich by dealing drugs, so you need territory and resources. You depend on the schools to market your drugs and to recruit new members. You depend on the corrupt government police to provide illegal weapons. In the past few weeks, the Kyats—your rival gang—have been winning more fights and getting more territory. They seem to have more weapons and more members. Last week twenty-three members of your gang were killed, including your leader. Will you fight again tonight? Who is going to lead you? If you fight without a leader, you're likely to lose more vital people. If you don't fight, you'll lose valuable territory, not to mention your reputation.

- -

Kyats

You're a gang member, and you shoot anyone for almost any reason. Your goal is to get rich by dealing drugs, so you need territory and resources. You depend on the schools to market your drugs and to recruit new members. You depend on the corrupt government police to provide illegal weapons. In the past few weeks, you've been gaining territory. The Sovalos—your rival gang—are losing members and you're dominating because a bad cop has given you access to a stash of illegal weapons and ammunition. But last night he was arrested before you could get supplies for tonight's battle, and you are dangerously low on supplies of ammunition. Will you fight tonight? Where will you get your weapons? If you fight without enough weapons, you'll probably get slaughtered. If you don't fight, you'll lose valuable territory, not to mention your reputation.

- -

Government

You've been struggling for years to solve your country's problems, which seem to get worse every week. Your goals are to keep control of the country and stop the violence. You're running out of money, and you're forced to make drastic cuts. Your choices are cutting the military's budget, cutting funding for the schools, or cutting your own paycheck. If you cut the military's budget, you'll be defenseless; if you cut the school budget, the teachers will strike and create more chaos; if you cut your own paycheck, your family could starve. Will you outlaw guns completely, leaving average citizens no way to defend themselves? Will you declare war on the gangs and bring in the military, risking a confrontation in which thousands will die?

School System

As a teacher, most of your former coworkers in public schools left the profession fearing for their lives. For one reason or another, you've decided to risk your life and remain in the classroom. Your goal is to create a safe environment for students. But while you try to teach, gangs roam the halls, selling drugs to your students and recruiting new members. Every teacher brings a gun to school—you depend on yours for self-defense. But the government is threatening to outlaw all guns, leaving you defenseless, and to cut your paycheck, leaving you no way to feed your family. Will you go on strike, giving up your paycheck altogether? Will you screen every student entering the school, risking direct hits on your life?

Public

You're scared to death. You may be a parent of a gang member; if so, you're afraid that your child will die or bring the violence into your home. You're powerless as an individual, but you can have great influence by joining with the rest of the Public to form a large group. You can decide to lobby in Congress for specific laws or volunteer with the police force or go straight to the gangs and try to change their ways. You can get involved with the School System and try to change the school environment. You can collectively decide a plan of attack, trying to get everyone in your group to agree, or you can split up into smaller groups. But always keep in mind your goals: to stay alive and to stop the violence.

It's Not **MY** Fault!

When Life Is Unfair

by Steve and Jenny Saavedra

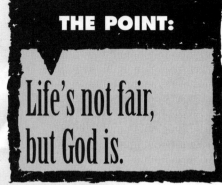

THE POINT:

Life's not fair, but God is.

■ "I'm a victim": It's our society's new mantra for a new millennium. The Menendez brothers used this as their primary defense in a California court where they were convicted for the murder of their parents. More recently, a fourteen-year-old girl stole a mail-order shipment of a muscle relaxant from a neighbor's porch. She passed the pills out at a dance, where more than a dozen students overdosed. Since, they have all recovered ("Teen girl charged in pill overdose," The Denver Post, March 11, 1997), but some people have blamed the pharmaceutical company for this episode. ■ John Leo, in a column for U.S. News & World Report, says: "Everything bad that happens to us is someone else's fault, and someone else must be made to pay…Football, for example, is a brutal game with plenty of head injuries, but those who get such injuries don't blame themselves or chalk it up to bad luck. They blame helmet manufacturers. So half the cost of a $200 helmet pays for manufacturer insurance" ("The world's most litigious nation," May 22, 1995). ■ But while the cry of victimization may seem to be growing louder than ever, casting blame is nothing new to the human experience. It dates back to the first page of human history. Adam blamed Eve for giving him fruit from the tree; Eve in turn blamed the serpent. The serpent had nothing left to blame…except his own degradation. And in the end, this is exactly what God's justice found in them all; he held them all personally responsible. ■ Even after thousands of years, we still think we can get off by blaming others. Teenagers are no different. But with Christian maturity comes the ability to take full responsibility for our actions when we're indeed at fault. And when life is unjust or we're blamed unfairly, Christian maturity also engenders a fundamental trust in God's justice and the grace to handle such situations appropriately. ■ This study starts your teenagers down this lifelong path by forcing them to grapple with unfair situations in real life. Kids can learn that unfair situations may grate against their sense of justice but that those situations challenge kids to think twice before casting blame or retaliating.

The Study
AT A GLANCE

SECTION	MINUTES	WHAT STUDENTS WILL DO	SUPPLIES
Unfair Situations	3 to 5	SHARE THE BLAME—Tell partners about unfair situations they're facing.	Newsprint, marker, tape
Anticipation Guide	15 to 20	GRAPPLE WITH GUSTO—Respond as individuals to four statements about unfair situations and then reach a consensus in small groups.	"Grapple With Gusto" handouts (p. 45), pencils or pens, newsprint, marker, tape
Scripture Study	10 to 15	REFERENCE RUMMAGING—Study Scriptures that relate to God's justice and unfair situations.	Bibles, "Reference Rummaging" handouts (p. 46), "Grapple With Gusto" handouts (p. 45), pencils or pens, newsprint, marker
Integrative Skits	10 to 15	TAG-TEAM DRAMA—Act out unfair situations that others conclude positively.	
Closing	3 to 5	FULL CIRCLE—Help partners discover solutions to unfair situations.	Bibles

notes:

Life's not fair, but God is.

THE BIBLE CONNECTION

PSALM 7	David agonizes over an unfair situation and appeals to God's justice for vindication.
NAHUM 1:2-3a	The prophet extols God's justice, citing that God will not leave the guilty unpunished.
LUKE 15:11-24	The prodigal son accepts the blame and responsibility for his actions, while the father shows love and mercy.
ROMANS 12:14-21	Paul prescribes ways to handle our enemies and unjust situations.

I n this study, kids will determine what their responses would be to four unfair situations and will explore Scripture to determine if their responses agree with God's guidance. Then kids will model responses to unjust situations through skits. Finally, kids will help partners determine personal and proper responses to unfair situations they're currently facing.

Through these experiences, kids can discover a biblical pattern for handling unfair situations and can learn that they can trust God's justice.

Explore the verses in The Bible Connection; then examine the information in the Depthfinder boxes throughout the study to gain a deeper understanding of how these Scriptures connect with your young people.

LEADER TIP for The Study

Because this topic can be so powerful and relevant to kids' lives, your group members may be tempted to get caught up in issues and lose sight of the deeper biblical principles found in The Point. Help your kids grasp The Point by guiding them to focus on the biblical investigation and by discussing how God's truth connects with reality in their lives.

BEFORE THE STUDY

For the "Share the Blame" activity, copy the following questions onto a sheet of newsprint, and tape up the newsprint so kids can refer to it during the activity.
● How does it feel to be blamed?
● Why do you think you're being blamed unfairly?
● What are you planning to do about this situation?
● Does anybody care that you're taking the heat for this? If so, who?
● Do you think God cares about what's happening to you right now? Why or why not?

Make one photocopy of the "Grapple With Gusto" handout (p. 45) for each student and one photocopy of the "Reference Rummaging" handout (p. 46) for each student. Also, draw a large version of the "Grapple With Gusto" handout (p. 45) on newsprint, and tape up the newsprint; it should be large enough to record responses so students can track how their classmates respond to each statement.

THE STUDY

UNFAIR SITUATIONS ▼

Share the Blame (3 to 5 minutes) Instruct each student to find a partner. Have kids tell their partners about situations they're currently facing in which they're being blamed unfairly. Ask kids to refer to the questions you wrote on newsprint before the study and discuss them with their partners.

After each pair discusses the questions, say: **I'm sure all of you can think of many other unfair situations. There's no shortage of them in life. And sometimes it's hard to know how to handle such situations. We know that <u>life's not fair, but God is.</u> Today we'll explore what it means to be Christians serving a fair God.**

ANTICIPATION GUIDE ▼

Grapple With Gusto (15 to 20 minutes) Give each student a copy of the "Grapple With Gusto" handout (p. 45) and a pencil or pen. Encourage each person to find space in the room to work on the handout privately and silently. Instruct kids to read each statement individually and then write in column 1 whether they agree or disagree with the statement. It's very important that kids not consult with others. Allow only three minutes for this activity.

Then have kids form groups of four or five. Say: **As a group, I want you to fill out column 2 on your handouts. It's important that you come to a unanimous group decision regarding each of the four statements. While you discuss the statements, don't listen to or interact with other groups.**

Allow no more than ten minutes for kids to wrestle with column 2; then have each group report its findings to the entire class. Write groups' responses on the newsprint version of the handout you prepared before the study so the class can track how each group responded. Then ask:

● **As you look at your classmates' responses for column 2, do you think the way they responded to the four statements is one hundred percent fair? Why or why not?**

Then say: **Sometimes it's very hard to make sense of the unfair situations we face in life. We know <u>life's not fair, but God is.</u> Let's look at what the Bible says about each of the statements on your handout.**

DEPTH FINDER
THE SKINNY ON GRAPPLING

The activity "Grapple With Gusto" is designed to get kids thinking about several fronts on the unfair "battleground" of life.

The first statement gets kids thinking about accepting responsibility when something is their fault—a difficult thing for people to do at any age. Learning to accept responsibility is not only an important life skill, but it's also essential to Christian living. Without the recognition and confession of personal sin, there can be no realization of the need for redemption.

The second statement stimulates thought about God's justice and whether God can be trusted to vindicate us when we're treated unfairly. It's vital for kids to recognize not only that there is a God, but also that there is a *personal* God who cares deeply about the injustices they face.

The third statement focuses on victimization and our society's tendency to blame our actions on the influence of others instead of taking full responsibility for ourselves. It's important for kids to develop critical thinking skills so they can recognize when the victimization mind-set crosses the line from legitimacy to absurdity. False victimization even raises its self-absolving head in Christian circles—for example, when people blame spirits or demons exclusively for deviant behaviors and attitudes that violate Christian principles.

Finally, the fourth statement gets kids thinking about how to respond to life's unfairness. It questions whether we should take justice into our own hands or simply trust God for our vindication, which may take a different shape than we expect. It's important for kids to realize that God is not a Santa Claus in the sky waiting to fulfill our every vindictive wish. Our wills and God's will are often at odds, and his justice may come at a time and in a way we don't expect or even hope for. But nevertheless, kids should be assured that God's justice will indeed come.

SCRIPTURE STUDY ▼

Reference Rummaging (10 to 15 minutes) Have kids stay in their groups. Give each student a copy of the "Reference Rummaging" handout (p. 46). Instruct groups to look up the Scriptures and answer the questions. Then in column 3 of kids' "Grapple With Gusto" handouts, have kids write whether they think the Bible agrees or disagrees with each statement. Again, encourage kids to reach a consensus in their groups.

When groups have finished, have them report their conclusions to the rest of the class. Again, record their responses on the newsprint version of the handout. Then ask:

● **What did you discover about God's fairness?**

● **Do you think life is more fair for Christians than for non-Christians? Why or why not?**

Then say: **Sometimes we feel we're being blamed unfairly. When that happens, it's important to ask God if we're at all responsible for what's happening, just as David did in Psalm 7. If we're responsible—even a little bit—the right thing to do is to admit it and not blame others, just as the prodigal son did in**

LEADER TIP
for Grapple With Gusto

It's important for the groups to struggle through the four statements to arrive at a group consensus. Don't let kids off the hook easily. During this section, kids may be tempted to go off on tangents or become hung up on certain statements. Keep kids on track and pace them. Limit discussions to two to three minutes per statement. If kids can't reach a consensus after this time, tell them it's OK for them to say they're undecided as long as they can explain why. Then encourage kids to move along.

The four statements are purposely designed to fall into "gray" areas to foster debate and active engagement with the issues. Kids may want or look for neat, tidy answers to the tough questions raised by the statements. Be prepared to help kids come to the conclusion that although life's not fair, God is.

DEPTH FINDER — TEMPERED JUSTICE

One dictionary defines "justice" as "reward or penalty as deserved" and "the quality of being righteous." God is certainly both just and righteous. Much of Old Testament law reflects God's passion for fairness and intolerance of evil. Old Testament law is based on the idea that humans should get what they deserve—an eye for an eye, and a life for a life.

But fortunately for us, God is not simply a just judge. God's justice is tempered by mercy. In his grace, he does nothing less than give us what we don't deserve. God's Word commands us to refuse to take revenge on our enemies (Romans 12:14-21); this command reflects God's grace and his merging of mercy and justice.

Help kids understand that God's justice doesn't always look like we think it should. It often takes on different shapes and forms, and it arrives at unexpected times. God's justice may arrive in this life as a tangible consequence, or it may be in the form of an unfulfilled life. God's justice may even be postponed until the final judgment.

Encourage kids to hold on to the promise that God's justice will prevail. Even though it can be hard to see God's justice in this world, we can trust in God's timing and "leave room for God's wrath" (Romans 12:19).

Luke 15. **But if we're really being blamed unfairly, we can be encouraged because God is fair. We can trust that God ultimately will not let people get away with treating us unfairly. Sometimes God's justice looks different from ours. God doesn't always respond how or when we want him to. But God does tell us how**  **we should respond: with love for our enemies and trust in God's justice. Life's not fair, but God is. He'll watch out for us. Now let's think about what this looks like in real life.**

INTEGRATIVE SKITS ▼

Tag-Team Drama (10 to 15 minutes)

Ask each group to think of an unfair situation from real life. The situation can be from the "Grapple With Gusto" handout, a personal situation mentioned at the beginning of class, or a purely hypothetical situation. Tell each group to plan a quick skit—no longer than one minute—that establishes an unfair situation but doesn't resolve it. All members of the group must participate.

Explain that groups will perform their dramas one at a time; then at the "height" of each unfair situation, the actors will freeze. Then one of the players will point to another group, indicating that the other group must complete the story. After a quick huddle to discuss how the drama should continue, the new group will assume the same positions and roles of the first and will perform an ending for the rest of the class.

Say: **The "concluding" group is free to make up any ending it wants as long as the ending demonstrates not only a proper human response to the unfair situation, but also God's justice**

DEPTHFINDER

THE GOOD PRODIGAL SON

The prodigal son in Luke 15 is not often considered a role model. But if we look at his humble, repentant heart at the end of Jesus' parable and compare it to the proud spirit and sense of entitlement he could have possessed, we may begin to see him in a new light.

It's easy to imagine that the prodigal son could have used a number of excuses for his predicament. He could have blamed his misfortune on friends who influenced and encouraged his destructive behavior. He easily could have blamed the famine for his undoing. He also could have blamed his employer for not rehabilitating him or giving him a better job, much less a decent meal. And he even could have blamed his family upbringing for not giving him the life skills to "make it" in the real world.

But when it came time for the prodigal son to go back home, he blamed no one but himself: "Father, I have sinned against heaven and against you" (verse 18). His contrite heart and his willingness to take responsibility for his actions shaped the end of the story. We usually neglect to imagine an ending containing anything other than the welcoming arms of a father. But imagine a rebellious, bitter son returning to blame everything under the sun for his circumstances. Without a repentant heart, would this prodigal have been relegated to the pig sty for the rest of his days?

working in the situation. Encourage kids to highlight in their skits new things they learned from the Bible study—for example, what it means to live as a Christian serving a fair God.

When the "concluding" group has finished the skit, have both groups take a bow while the rest of the class says together, "Life's not fair, but God is." Discuss each drama by asking the class the following questions:

● **What would've been an improper way to respond to this situation?**

● **How was God's fairness revealed in this drama?**

When all the skits have been performed and concluded, ask:

● **How did you react when you saw God looking out for the characters in these dramas?**

● **For the groups that ended skits, how was this experience like trying to solve problems of injustice in real life?**

● **How did it feel to "jump in" and make decisions that corrected unfair situations?**

CLOSING ▼

Full Circle (3 to 5 minutes)
Say: **Many unfair situations will come your way. Life's not fair, but God is. As Christians, we should respond to unfair situations in a way that shows that we know God sees injustice and won't let evil win.**

Instruct students to find their partners from the beginning of class. Tell partners to help each other come up with solutions to their personal unfair situations. Encourage kids to think of practical ways to respond, fully taking into consideration the fact that there is a fair God.

To close the meeting, instruct the students to read Psalm 7:1-10 to their partners and then say, "I know that you can overcome unfairness God's way, with God's help."

Then have the kids form a circle. Lead the students in prayer, asking God to show them how his fairness and justice acts in their lives.

"The Lord is slow to anger and great in power; the Lord will not leave the guilty unpunished."

—Nahum 1:3a

Grapple With **Gusto**

Read the following four statements. In column 1, write either "A" for agree or "D" for disagree. For now, leave column 2 and column 3 blank. Be ready to give reasons why you agree or disagree with each statement.

Column 1 (You)	Column 2 (Group)	Column 3 (Bible)	
_____	_____	_____	1. If somebody accuses you of doing something you don't remember doing, you shouldn't even think about taking the responsibility.
_____	_____	_____	2. God sometimes lets people get away with cheating.
_____	_____	_____	3. You asked your parents for help on an assignment, but they didn't have time. You ended up getting a bad grade. It's your parents' fault.
_____	_____	_____	4. When someone insults you at school, you should never let the person get away with it. God expects us to stand up for ourselves.

Reference **Rummaging**

1. Read Psalm 7:1-5, and then discuss the following questions with your group:

- David (the author) found himself in an unfair situation. Based on these verses, did David think he was guilty or innocent?
- Do you think David was ready to take the responsibility for his actions if he was really guilty? Why or why not?
- Would David agree or disagree with the first statement on the "Grapple With Gusto" handout? Write down your answer in column 3.

2. Read Psalm 7:6-17 and Nahum 1:2-3a, and then discuss the following questions with your group:

- On the back of this handout, list eight things these verses say about God and what he does.
- In Psalm 7:14-16, what did David say would happen to people who do wrong? Do you think that's fair? Why or why not?
- Based on these verses, do you think the Bible supports or contradicts the second statement on the "Grapple With Gusto" handout? Write your answer in column 3.

3. Read Luke 15:11-24, and then discuss the following questions with your group:

- Who and what could the character in the story blame his misfortune on? List three things on the back of this handout.
- Who did the son blame for his misfortune?
- Why didn't the father give the son what he seemed to deserve? Why didn't he just let his son suffer the consequences?
- The father in the story represents God. What does this story say about God's justice?
- Do you think the son in this story would agree or disagree with the third statement on the "Grapple With Gusto" handout? Write your answer in column 3.

4. Read Romans 12:14-21, and then discuss the following questions with your group:

- Do you think God's idea of justice is different from ours? If so, how?
- How does this Scripture passage recommend we deal with people who treat us unfairly?
- Why do you think God wants us to respond this way? What's difficult about responding this way?
- Does the Bible support or contradict the fourth statement on the "Grapple With Gusto" handout? Write your answer in column 3.

This Is What *Love* Is
Showing God's True Love

by Mikal Keefer

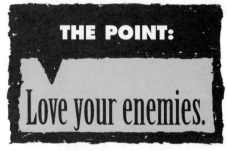

THE POINT:

Love your enemies.

■ Enemies... ■ Your kids are old enough to have them. They may be as fleeting as a classmate who taunts a girl about a "bad hair day," and as permanent as an abusive parent. There's nothing rare about having enemies, but there *can* be something extraordinary about how your kids deal with their enemies. ■ Jesus told his followers to respond to enemies not with a fist, but with compassion. It may be the least natural response, but Jesus didn't give his followers an option. And Jesus not only talked about it; he also demonstrated how to do it. ■ Why did Jesus insist we give our tormentors such a break? And how do we manage to show compassion when our first instinct is to strike back at anyone who takes a swing at us? ■ This study will help kids explore strategies for handling enemies and discover how to respond in ways that can turn most enemies into friends. By learning how to feel and express compassion, your kids will not only become more heartfelt followers of Jesus, but they'll also discover that their world stretches past their own personal concerns. They'll discover that they can impact others—and their world—in a positive way.

The Study
AT A GLANCE

SECTION	MINUTES	WHAT STUDENTS WILL DO	SUPPLIES
Introductory Activity	10 to 15	COMPASSION RATIONS—Identify stories about enemies in magazines and newspapers and then contrast most people's response to enemies with the way Jesus wants us to respond.	Bible, newspapers, magazines, newsprint, marker, tape
Bible Exploration	10 to 15	ENEMIES: YA GOTTA LOVE 'EM—Discuss where enemies come from and consider how group members have contributed to the supply.	Bibles, newsprint, marker, tape
Application Activity	15 to 20	SOMEONE'S GOTTA PAY!—Play a "TV game show" and discover that there's a cost for forgiveness and compassion.	Bible, paper, markers, "Someone's Gotta Pay!" handout (p. 56), video camera and videotape (optional)
Application Discussion	8 to 10	AGREE OR DISAGREE—Decide whether they agree or disagree with statements about forgiveness and compassion.	Pennies, two buckets, paper, tape, marker
Directed Prayer	3 to 5	LETTING GO—Release anger about specific enemies and plan compassionate acts or words they can share.	Buckets or tarp, stones or bricks, pebbles

notes:

Love your enemies.

THE BIBLE CONNECTION

MATTHEW 5:23-24	Jesus describes the priority God places on healing damaged relationships, and Christians' responsibility for taking the first step.
MATTHEW 5:43-48	Jesus describes one way Christians should be different from others: We should love our enemies.
LUKE 6:27-36	Jesus speaks some shocking words about a new way to treat enemies.

I n this study, kids will identify types of enemies they may have, explore what Jesus says about loving enemies and showing compassion, recognize the cost of compassion, and decide if they're willing to be compassionate to specific enemies.

By doing this, teenagers can learn to put into practice the same kind of compassionate love Jesus has shown us.

Explore the verses in The Bible Connection; then examine the information in the Depthfinder boxes throughout the study to gain a deeper understanding of how these Scriptures connect with your young people.

LEADER TIP
for The Study

Whenever groups discuss a list of questions, write the list on newsprint and tape the newsprint to a wall so groups can discuss the questions at their own pace.

BEFORE THE STUDY

For the "Compassion Rations" activity, stack old newspapers and magazines in the middle of the room. Copy the lists of discussion questions for the "Compassion Rations" and "Enemies: Ya Gotta Love 'Em" activities onto a piece of newsprint, and tape the newsprint to a wall. Using paper and a marker, create two labels to tape to two buckets. Label one bucket "Agree" and another bucket "Disagree."

LEADER TIP

for The Study

Because this topic can be so powerful and relevant to kids' lives, your group members may be tempted to get caught up in issues and lose sight of the deeper biblical principles found in The Point. Help your kids grasp The Point by guiding them to focus on the biblical investigation and by discussing how God's truth connects with reality in their lives.

THE STUDY

INTRODUCTORY ACTIVITY ▼

Compassion Rations (10 to 15 minutes)

As kids arrive, ask them to form groups of three. Then show students the stack of newspapers and magazines.

Say: **In your group, use these newspapers and magazines to find a story about enemies. For example, you might find a story about armies attacking each other, a woman battered by her estranged husband, or politicians trashing each other while running for office. Be ready to share your story with the other groups.**

After five minutes, ask each group to present a thirty-second report that includes answers to these questions, which you wrote on newsprint before the study:

● Who are the enemies in your story?
● Why are the enemies at odds?
● What would it take for the enemies to become friends?

When groups have given their reports, say: **There's no shortage of enemies in the world. Every one of us has at least one enemy—someone who treats us poorly or looks down on us. Usually our first inclination is to give our enemies the same grief they give us, but that's not how Jesus requires that we respond to enemies.**

Read Luke 6:27-36 aloud.

Ask kids to discuss these questions, which you wrote on newsprint before the study, in their groups:

● If you were one of the enemies in your story, could you do as Jesus demands? Why or why not?

● If the enemies in your story were loving to each other, how would they behave?

● Describe a time when you've been compassionate toward someone who treated you poorly. Was it difficult to be compassionate? Explain.

When groups have discussed the questions, say: **It's easy to find examples of how enemies treat each other, but it can be hard to find examples of people doing what Jesus said to do: Love your enemies.**

Let's find out more about what Jesus has commanded us to do.

BIBLE EXPLORATION ▼

Enemies: Ya Gotta Love 'Em (10 to 15 minutes)

Say: **Let's talk about enemies. Some enemies are "situation" enemies. Suppose we're soldiers, and your country declares war on my country. We automatically** become enemies. It's nothing personal, but we're still shooting at each other.

Other enemies are "personal" enemies—people who dislike us *personally.* Maybe they don't like our ethnic background, the way we talk, or where we're from. Maybe they dislike our Christian faith.

It's possible to have an enemy even though you've done nothing to hurt the other person.

Have kids form pairs and discuss these questions, which you wrote on newsprint before the study, with their partners:

● When have you realized that someone, for no good reason, just didn't like you?

● How did that feel?

● How did you treat that person?

● Was there something you could have done about the situation?

Ask partners to read aloud Matthew 5:43-48 and discuss these questions, which you wrote on newsprint before the study:

● How does Jesus say to treat enemies?

● How could you apply Jesus' words to the situation you've described?

● If you rated yourself on how you love your enemies ("ten" means "perfect," and "one" means "not at all"), how would you rate? Explain.

● If you were to pray for your enemies, what would you pray for?

When pairs have discussed the questions, say: **Sometimes a person may become your enemy because of something you've done. Maybe you accidentally put a rock through someone's window, maybe you gossiped about someone, or maybe you lost someone's autographed Michael Jordan jersey. You messed up, and someone dislikes you for it. Maybe that person is even trying to harm you.**

Instruct students to find new partners and discuss these questions, which you wrote on newsprint before the study:

● When have you had an enemy—at least for a while—because of something you did?

● How did that feel?

● How did that person treat you?

● How did you treat that person?

● Was there something you could have done to help the situation?

Ask partners to read aloud Matthew 5:23-24 and discuss these questions, which you wrote on newsprint before the study:

● What did Jesus say to do when you've created an enemy?

● How could you apply Jesus' words to the situation you've described?

● What's the connection between your relationship with God and your relationships with your enemies?

● What can you do if your enemy doesn't show you compassion by reconciling with you?

Say: **Jesus made it clear that we're responsible for how we treat our enemies. It's our job to show them compassion and love—no matter how they treat us. We're to treat enemies with warmth; respect; and empathy, which means we're to see things from their perspective as well as our own. We should share our resources of time, energy, and materials and should look out for our enemies' best interests.** Ask:

● **What are practical ways you can show love and compassion to your enemies?**

● **Think specifically about a person who has treated you poorly. Without naming names, what does that person need in his or her life? How can you help provide it?**

● **Does Jesus' command to <u>love your enemies</u> make sense to you? Why or why not?**

APPLICATION ACTIVITY ▼

Someone's Gotta Pay! (15 to 20 minutes)

LEADER TIP

for Someone's Gotta Pay!

Use these prices as benchmarks to determine which team is closest to an accurate price: The bike costs $1,204; the computer costs $2,520; the dental work costs $2,600.

Someone's Gotta Pay! You may want to arrange to have someone videotape this activity. It's not necessary for the completion of the study, but it can add to the fun.

Have kids form teams of three or four. Say: **Now we're going to play "Someone's Gotta Pay," an exciting new game show that lets contestants be judge and jury in deciding how much to award a person who's been wronged.**

Give each team paper and a marker. Say: **I'll describe several situations and will ask you a question about each one. After I ask you the question, you'll have one minute to come to a decision as a team and write your answer on the paper I've given you.**

Read aloud the "Round 1" section from the "Someone's Gotta Pay!" handout (p. 56). Then give teams sixty seconds to write answers.

After one minute, ask teams to display their papers. Award five hundred points to the team whose amount is closest to the true amount.

Continue to read the situations described on the "Someone's Gotta Pay!" handout. For each round, award five hundred points to the team whose guess is closest to the actual amount. In rounds 4 and 5, require teams to explain and justify their answers. Award the points to the team that guesses the highest number or the greatest sacrifice.

After round 5, award "bonus points" for qualifications such as style, good sportsmanship, and best-tied shoelaces to every team except the team in the lead. Add enough points to each team's score so that each team ends up with the exact same amount of points—making everyone a winner!

When the game is over, ask:

- ● **What was easy about playing this game? What was difficult?**
- ● **What was it like to put a price on people's suffering?**
- ● **What was it like to compete with another team?**
- ● **How was that similar to having an enemy? How was it different?**
- ● **How did you feel at the end of the game when everyone had the same number of points and everyone won?**
- ● **How was that similar to having compassion for an enemy? How was it different?**
- ● **How was that similar to what Jesus has done for us?**

Say: **Our society believes people should pay for mistakes. We're quick to place blame and demand payment when we've been wronged.**

But when you forgive, you pay for the mistake of someone else yourself. If Dana forgives the driver who crushed her new bike, she's out the money it costs to replace the bike. If the school forgives Alfie, the school has to pay to replace the computer.

No amount of money could really pay for six months of torture. And how could we repay Jesus for what he gave us on the cross? There isn't anything we can do to square the debt we owe.

When we have compassion on our enemies and show them love by forgiving them, we let go of our rights to demand payment or revenge. We do for our enemies what Jesus has done for us.

When we love our enemies, we deliberately seek to do good for our enemies. We move past grudging tolerance to full acceptance. And we become Christlike in our actions and attitudes.

Read Luke 6:27-36 aloud and ask:

- ● **How is what Jesus asks us to do for our enemies like what he did for his enemies? How is it different?**
- ● **What will it cost to treat enemies the way Jesus wants?**
- ● **What's the benefit of treating our enemies this way?**
- ● **Jesus showed his love and compassion for his enemies by dying for us. How can you specifically show love for your enemies?**

Say: **When someone commits a wrong, that person owes a debt. When you act with compassion by forgiving an enemy, you <u>love your enemies.</u>**

LEADER TIP for Someone's Gotta Pay!

If you videotaped the game show, serve popcorn and play the videotape. Kids are no different from adults: They love to see themselves on TV. And watching the video provides an opportunity to reinforce The Point: Love your enemies.

LEADER TIP for Someone's Gotta Pay!

If you hear howls of protest from the game "winners" about the "losers" being given an equal reward, consider pausing to investigate Jesus' parable in Matthew 20:1-16.

APPLICATION DISCUSSION ▼

Agree or Disagree (8 to 10 minutes) Have kids form a circle and sit on the floor. Give each person four pennies. Place the two buckets you labeled before the study on the floor in the middle of the circle.

Say: **I'm going to read a passage from the book *Strength to Love* by Martin Luther King Jr. If you agree with him, place one penny in the "agree" bucket. If you disagree, place one penny in the "disagree" bucket. Then return to your spot.**

"Forgiveness does not mean ignoring what has been done or

putting a false label on an evil act. It means, rather, that the evil act no longer remains as a barrier to the relationship… Forgiveness means reconciliation, a coming together again. Without this, no man can love his enemies."

Instruct students to place their pennies in the buckets. Then have kids form groups of three and explain why they agreed or disagreed. After groups have had two minutes to talk, ask volunteers to share insights from their group discussions. Then have kids form a circle again.

Say: **Consider this statement: You can hate your enemies and still act compassionately toward them. If you agree, place one penny in the "agree" bucket. If you disagree, place one penny in the "disagree" bucket.**

Ask kids to form different groups of three and explain why they agreed or disagreed. After groups have had two minutes to talk, ask volunteers to share insights. Then have kids form a circle again.

Say: **Consider this statement: When you can see things through the eyes of your enemy, you're halfway to solving your problem. If you agree, place one penny in the "agree" bucket. If you disagree, place one penny in the "disagree" bucket.**

Ask kids to form different groups of three and explain why they agreed or disagreed. After groups have had two minutes to talk, ask volunteers to share insights. Then have kids form a circle again.

Say: **Consider this statement: I am willing to do what Jesus says and deliberately forgive and act compassionately toward someone who has wronged me. I will act in a loving way even if I don't feel like loving that person. I will begin this week to love an enemy.**

If you're willing to begin loving an enemy this week, place one penny in the "agree" bucket. If you're not willing, place one penny in the "disagree" bucket.

Have kids form different groups of three and explain why they agreed or disagreed. After trios have had two minutes to talk, ask kids to take turns praying in their groups for the people sitting on their left.

Say: **Your intentions to love your enemies don't mean much without action. Let's begin now to take some action.**

DIRECTED PRAYER ▼

Letting Go (3 to 5 minutes)
Give each teenager a very small pebble and a fist-sized stone or a brick. Ask teenagers to stand in a circle and face toward the center of the circle, holding their stones or bricks and their pebbles. Place buckets or a tarp (to protect the floor) in the center of the circle.

Say: **In biblical times, one way people punished enemies and criminals was by crushing their skulls and bones by throwing stones at them. I confess that there have been times when I have hated my enemies, sometimes for reasons that feel trivial to me now.**

I suspect we've all felt tremendous anger toward an enemy. Maybe you're feeling it now. Take a moment to think of someone you would define as an enemy in your life.

DEPTH FINDER

MORE ABOUT LOVE AND COMPASSION

Try these ideas to teach your teenagers more about what it means to have compassion and to love enemies.

● Have kids identify a group of people they would consider an enemy. Maybe it's a political group such as the Ku Klux Klan or an economic group such as the wealthy. Have kids think about what they could do to communicate compassion and love to those specific people. Encourage them to think about how they could show love and compassion as a group. Then help them carry out those actions.

● The courts have decreed a number of individuals enemies of the people. Prisons, jails, and juvenile detention centers are full of such people. Contact your nearest detention facility, and find out how you can communicate compassion to the people there. Be aware that there may be nonnegotiable rules governing personal visits, and correspondence may be dangerous. Contact a prison ministry organization or talk to a prison chaplain to discover what your options are.

● Have teenagers form two groups. Read Matthew 25:31-46 aloud, and ask the two groups to work together to pantomime the interaction before God's throne. Then have students discuss questions like these: How did it feel to be in your group? How does treating your enemies compassionately figure into this story? What can you do to live compassionately in each of the areas Jesus listed?

Pause for several moments, and then say: **I'd like each of you to have a chance to let go of your anger so you can act with compassion toward your enemy. Perhaps you need to forgive an enemy, do what's best for your enemy, try to see things from your enemy's point of view, or begin to treat your enemy with respect.**

In a moment, I'm going to say, "Because of what Jesus has done for me, I will love my enemy." Then I'll move to the center of the circle and release my stone as I release my anger. If you're willing to release your anger toward an enemy and give up your desire to hurt an enemy, please repeat after me and then do as I do. If you don't feel comfortable with this commitment, it's OK to just spend the time praying, asking God to help you come to the point where you can love your enemy.

Walk to the middle of the circle as you say: **Because of what Jesus has done for me, I will love my enemy.** Then drop your stone into a bucket or onto the tarp.

When everyone who wants to has had a chance to repeat after you, pray aloud. Thank God for the courage of the kids who released their anger and for the honesty of the kids who didn't release their stones. Ask God to show kids how to move toward lives of compassion and love for their enemies. Thank God for the example set by Jesus.

After your prayer, say: **Please place the pebble you're still holding in your shoe. Leave it there until you've done what you decided to do to show love to your enemy—or until you've taken a step toward letting go of your anger and loving an enemy. This pebble can be a reminder that you've been forgiven so much by Jesus and that you can share a tiny bit of that compassion with another person.**

LEADER TIP
for Letting Go

Your kids may have good reasons to be angry. Maybe they're being abused, or perhaps they're suffering in another ongoing, unjust situation. Don't demand that they release their stones, and affirm kids even if they don't. But be sure to follow up and provide a listening ear. Your kids need to know that you care about what they're going through. Help them resolve their situations, or refer them to someone who can.

Someone's Gotta Pay!

Round 1

A careless driver spilled coffee on his lap while he was cruising through a neighborhood. His car jumped over the curb and crushed the new dual-suspension, Specialized, twenty-four-speed mountain bike Dana left parked outside the Yummy-Freeze. Someone's gotta pay! What will it cost the driver to replace Dana's bike?

Round 2

While he was playing computer games on the school's new NEC Versa 2630CD, 1.44 gig hard-drive laptop computer, Alfie Goldfarb let loose with one of his cataclysmic sneezes and blew the computer across a table and out a third-floor window. When it hit the sidewalk, there wasn't enough computer left to solder together a calculator. Someone's gotta pay! What will it cost Alfie to replace the laptop?

Round 3

Shelia *knew* she shouldn't sneak up and fire a snowball at the back of Jeff's head...but she did. Jeff turned at exactly the wrong moment, and the snowball knocked out his two front teeth. Now Jeff needs a dental bridge. Someone's gotta pay! How much money should Sheila give Jeff?

Round 4

When Denise moved to Malvia she felt safe...until the government fell and she was taken hostage. She was imprisoned and beaten for nearly six months, then suddenly released when Malvia's military dictator was overthrown. Her former captors are now coming to trial. Someone's gotta pay! How should they pay Denise for her experience?

Round 5

God sent his only Son to earth to live with us—the King of the Universe living with people who didn't deserve help. In fact, we were sinners and therefore had made ourselves enemies of God by rejecting him and turning away from him. Jesus provided an example of how to treat enemies by letting us kill him—willingly dying in our place—to pay the price of our sin. Someone's gotta pay! What price should we pay God for what we put Jesus through?

why ▼ Active and Interactive Learning works with teenagers

Let's Start With the Big Picture

Think back to a major life lesson you've learned.
Got it? Now answer these questions:
● Did you learn your lesson from something you read?
● Did you learn it from something you heard?
● Did you learn it from something you experienced?

If you're like 99 percent of your peers, you answered "yes" only to the third question—you learned your life lesson from something you experienced.

This simple test illustrates the most convincing reason for using active and interactive learning with young people: People learn best through experience. Or to put it even more simply, people learn by doing.

Learning by doing is what active learning is all about. No more sitting quietly in chairs and listening to a speaker expound theories about God—that's passive learning. Active learning gets kids out of their chairs and into the experience of life. With active learning, kids get to *do* what they're studying. They *feel* the effects of the principles you teach. They *learn* by experiencing truth firsthand.

Active learning works because it recognizes three basic learning needs and uses them in concert to enable young people to make discoveries on their own and to find practical life applications for the truths they believe.

So what are these three basic learning needs?
1. Teenagers need action.
2. Teenagers need to think.
3. Teenagers need to talk.

Read on to find out exactly how these needs will be met by using the active and interactive learning techniques in Group's Core Belief Bible Study Series in your youth group.

1. Teenagers Need Action

Aircraft pilots know well the difference between passive and active learning. Their passive learning comes through listening to flight instructors and reading flight-instruction books. Their active learning comes through actually flying an airplane or flight simulator. Books and lectures may be helpful, but pilots really learn to fly by manipulating a plane's controls themselves.

We can help young people learn in a similar way. Though we may engage students passively in some reading and listening to teachers, their understanding and application of God's Word will really take off through simulated and real-life experiences.

Forms of active learning include simulation games; role-plays; service projects; experiments; research projects; group pantomimes; mock trials; construction projects; purposeful games; field trips; and, of course, the most powerful form of active learning—real-life experiences.

We can more fully explain active learning by exploring four of its characteristics:

● **Active learning is an adventure.** Passive learning is almost always predictable. Students sit passively while the teacher or speaker follows a planned outline or script.

In active learning, kids may learn lessons the teacher never envisioned. Because the leader trusts students to help create the learning experience, learners may venture into unforeseen discoveries. And often the teacher learns as much as the students.

● **Active learning is fun and captivating.** What are we communicating when we say, "OK, the fun's over—time to talk about God"? What's the hidden message? That joy is separate from God? And that learning is separate from joy?

What a shame.

Active learning is not joyless. One seventh-grader we interviewed clearly remembered her best Sunday school lesson: "Jesus was the light, and we went into a dark room and shut off the lights. We had a candle, and we learned that Jesus is the light and the dark can't shut off the light." That's active learning. Deena enjoyed the lesson. She had fun. And she learned.

Active learning intrigues people. Whether they find a foot-washing experience captivating or maybe a bit uncomfortable, they learn. And they learn on a level deeper than any work sheet or teacher's lecture could ever reach.

● **Active learning involves everyone.** Here the difference between passive and active learning becomes abundantly clear. It's like the difference between watching a football game on television and actually playing in the game.

The "trust walk" provides a good example of involving everyone in active learning. Half of the group members put on blindfolds; the other half serve as guides. The "blind" people trust the guides to lead them through the building or outdoors. The guides prevent the blind people from falling down stairs or tripping over rocks. Everyone needs to participate to learn the inherent lessons of trust, faith, doubt, fear, confidence, and servanthood. Passive spectators of this experience would learn little, but participants learn a great deal.

● **Active learning is focused through debriefing.** Activity simply for activity's sake doesn't usually result in good learning. Debriefing—evaluating an experience by discussing it in pairs or small groups—helps focus the experience and draw out its meaning. Debriefing helps sort and order the information students gather during the experience. It helps learners relate the recently experienced activity to their lives.

The process of debriefing is best started immediately after an experience. We use a three-step process in debriefing: reflection, interpretation, and application.

Reflection—This first step asks the students, "How did you feel?" Active-learning experiences typically evoke an emotional reaction, so it's appropriate to begin debriefing at that level.

Some people ask, "What do feelings have to do with education?" Feelings have everything to do with education. Think back again to that time in your life when you learned a big lesson. In all likelihood, strong feelings accompanied that lesson. Our emotions tend to cement things into our memories.

When you're debriefing, use open-ended questions to probe feelings. Avoid questions that can be answered with a "yes" or "no." Let your learners know that there are no wrong answers to these "feeling" questions. Everyone's feelings are valid.

Interpretation—The next step in the debriefing process asks, "What does this mean to you? How is this experience like or unlike some other aspect of your life?" Now you're asking people to identify a message or principle from the experience.

You want your learners to discover the message for themselves. So instead of telling students your answers, take the time to ask questions that encourage self-discovery. Use Scripture and discussion in pairs or small groups to explore how the actions and effects of the activity might translate to their lives.

Alert! Some of your people may interpret wonderful messages that you never intended. That's not failure! That's the Holy Spirit at work. God allows us to catch different glimpses of his kingdom even when we all look through the same glass.

Application—The final debriefing step asks, "What will you do about it?" This step moves learning into action. Your young people have shared a common experience. They've discovered a principle. Now they must create something new with what they've just experienced and interpreted. They must integrate the message into their lives.

The application stage of debriefing calls for a decision. Ask your students how they'll change, how they'll grow, what they'll do as a result of your time together.

2. Teenagers Need to Think

Today's students have been trained not to think. They aren't dumber than previous generations. We've simply conditioned them not to use their heads.

You see, we've trained our kids to respond with the simplistic answers they think the teacher wants to hear. Fill-in-the-blank student workbooks and teachers who ask dead-end questions such as "What's the capital of Delaware?" have produced kids and adults who have learned not to think.

And it doesn't just happen in junior high or high school. Our children are schooled very early not to think. Teachers attempt to help kids read with nonsensical fill-in-the-blank drills, word scrambles, and missing-letter puzzles.

Helping teenagers think requires a paradigm shift in how we teach. We need to plan for and set aside time for higher-order thinking and be willing to reduce our time spent on lower-order parroting. Group's Core Belief Bible Study Series is designed to help you do just that.

Thinking classrooms look quite different from traditional classrooms. In most church environments, the teacher does most of the talking and hopes that knowledge will transmit from his or her brain to the students'. In thinking settings, the teacher coaches students to ponder, wonder, imagine, and problem-solve.

3. Teenagers Need to Talk

Everyone knows that the person who learns the most in any class is the teacher. Explaining a concept to someone else is usually more helpful to the explainer than to the listener. So why not let the students do more teaching? That's one of the chief benefits of letting kids do the talking. This process is called interactive learning.

What is interactive learning? Interactive learning occurs when students discuss and work cooperatively in pairs or small groups.

Interactive learning encourages learners to work together. It honors the fact that students can learn from one another, not just from the teacher. Students work together in pairs or small groups to accomplish shared goals. They build together, discuss together, and present together. They teach each other and learn from one another. Success as a group is celebrated. Positive interdependence promotes individual and group learning.

Interactive learning not only helps people learn but also helps learners feel better about themselves and get along better with others. It accomplishes these things more effectively than the independent or competitive methods.

Here's a selection of interactive learning techniques that are used in Group's Core Belief Bible Study Series. With any of these models, leaders may assign students to specific partners or small groups. This will maximize cooperation and learning by preventing all the "rowdies" from linking up. And it will allow for new friendships to form outside of established cliques.

Following any period of partner or small-group work, the leader may reconvene the entire class for large-group processing. During this time the teacher may ask for reports or discoveries from individuals or teams. This technique builds in accountability for the teacherless pairs and small groups.

Pair-Share—With this technique each student turns to a partner and responds to a question or problem from the teacher or leader. Every learner responds. There are no passive observers. The teacher may then ask people to share their partners' responses.

Study Partners—Most curricula and most teachers call for Scripture passages to be read to the whole class by one person. One reads; the others doze.

Why not relinquish some teacher control and let partners read and react with each other? They'll all be involved—and will learn more.

Learning Groups—Students work together in small groups to create a model, design artwork, or study a passage or story; then they discuss what they learned through the experience. Each person in the learning group may be assigned a specific role. Here are some examples:

Reader

Recorder (makes notes of key thoughts expressed during the reading or discussion)

Checker (makes sure everyone understands and agrees with answers arrived at by the group)

Encourager (urges silent members to share their thoughts)

When everyone has a specific responsibility, knows what it is, and contributes to a small group, much is accomplished and much is learned.

Summary Partners—One student reads a paragraph, then the partner summarizes the paragraph or interprets its meaning. Partners alternate roles with each paragraph.

The paraphrasing technique also works well in discussions. Anyone who wishes to share a thought must first paraphrase what the previous person said. This sharpens listening skills and demonstrates the power of feedback communication.

Jigsaw—Each person in a small group examines a different concept, Scripture, or part of an issue. Then each teaches the others in the group. Thus, all members teach, and all must learn the others' discoveries. This technique is called a jigsaw because individuals are responsible to their group for different pieces of the puzzle.

JIGSAW EXAMPLE

Here's an example of a jigsaw.

Assign four-person teams. Have teammates each number off from one to four. Have all the Ones go to one corner of the room, all the Twos to another corner, and so on.

Tell team members they're responsible for learning information in their numbered corners and then for teaching their team members when they return to their original teams.

Give the following assignments to various groups:

Ones: Read Psalm 22. Discuss and list the prophecies made about Jesus.

Twos: Read Isaiah 52:13–53:12. Discuss and list the prophecies made about Jesus.

Threes: Read Matthew 27:1-32. Discuss and list the things that happened to Jesus.

Fours: Read Matthew 27:33-66. Discuss and list the things that happened to Jesus.

After the corner groups meet and discuss, instruct all learners to return to their original teams and report what they've learned. Then have each team determine which prophecies about Jesus were fulfilled in the passages from Matthew.

Call on various individuals in each team to report one or two prophecies that were fulfilled.

You Can Do It Too!

All this information may sound revolutionary to you, but it's really not. God has been using active and interactive learning to teach his people for generations. Just look at Abraham and Isaac, Jacob and Esau, Moses and the Israelites, Ruth and Boaz. And then there's Jesus, who used active learning all the time!

Group's Core Belief Bible Study Series makes it easy for you to use active and interactive learning with your group. The active and interactive elements are automatically built in! Just follow the outlines, and watch as your kids grow through experience and positive interaction with others.

FOR DEEPER STUDY

For more information on incorporating active and interactive learning into your work with teenagers, check out these resources:

● *Why Nobody Learns Much of Anything at Church: And How to Fix It,* by Thom and Joani Schultz (Group Publishing) and
● *Do It! Active Learning in Youth Ministry,* by Thom and Joani Schultz (Group Publishing).

your evaluation of

Bible Study Series
for junior high/middle school

the truth about
GOD'S JUSTICE

Group Publishing, Inc.
Attention: Core Belief Talk-Back
P.O. Box 481
Loveland, CO 80539
Fax: (970) 669-1994

Please help us continue to provide innovative and useful resources for ministry. After you've led the studies in this volume, take a moment to fill out this evaluation; then mail or fax it to us at the address above. Thanks!

● ● ● ● ● ●

1. As a whole, this book has been (circle one)

not very helpful   very helpful
1   2   3   4   5   6   7   8   9   10

2. The best things about this book:

3. How this book could be improved:

4. What I will change because of this book:

5. Would you be interested in field-testing future Core Belief Bible Studies and giving us your feedback? If so, please complete the information below:

Name _____

Street address _____

City _____ State _____ Zip _____

Daytime telephone (____) _____ Date _____

THANKS!